A Taste
of culture

W9-BRL-737

FOODS OF JAPAN

Barbara Sheen

KIDHAVEN PRESS
An imprint of Thomson Gale, a part of The Thomson Corporation

THOMSON
★
GALE

Detroit • New York • San Francisco • San Diego • New Haven, Conn. • Waterville, Maine • London • Munich

THOMSON

━━━━ ✦ ━━━━ ™

GALE

LIBRARY OF CONGRESS CATALOGING-IN-PUBLICATION DATA
Sheen, Barbara.
Foods of Japan / by Barbara Sheen.
p. cm. — (A taste of culture)
Includes bibliographical references and index.
ISBN 0-7377-3035-8 (lib. : alk. paper)
1. Cookery, Japanese. I. Title. II. Series.
TX724.5.J3S438 2005
641.5952—dc22
2005003192

Contents

The Roots of Japanese Cooking

Japanese cooking is simple, elegant, and delicious. It includes only the freshest ingredients. Fish pulled wiggling from the ocean and rice and soybeans grown in Japanese soil are the roots of Japanese cooking.

Rice: A Gift from the Gods

Rice is the centerpiece of every Japanese meal. To the Japanese, *gohan*, the word for cooked rice, does not mean only cooked rice. It refers to the meal itself. "Go-han desu," which is Japanese for "Let's eat rice," is the way the Japanese say, "Let's eat!" In Japan no meal is complete without rice. In fact the average Japanese person eats 0.5 pound (0.23 kilogram) of rice a day.

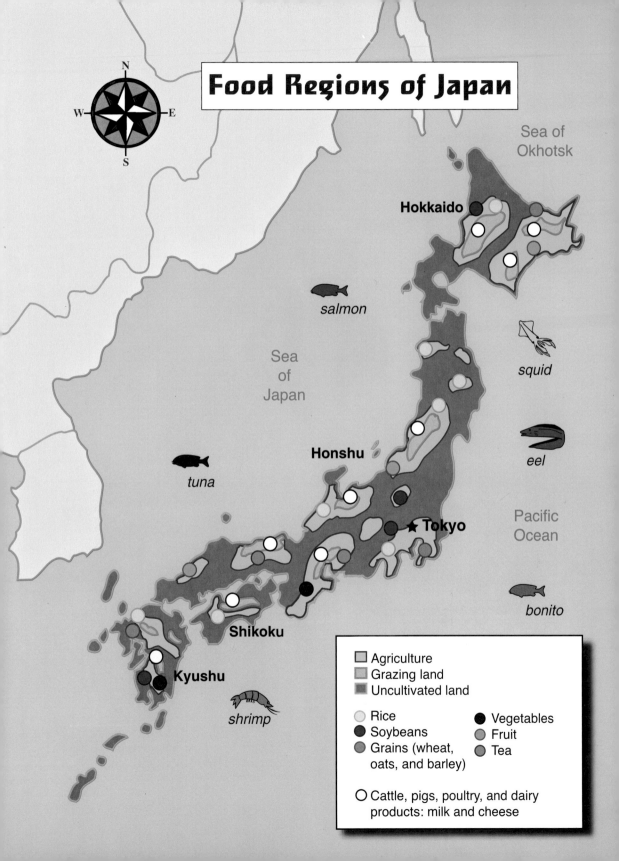

A Japanese woman dressed in a kimono prepares a tray of rice and fish dishes, with hot tea to drink.

The Japanese have been eating rice for more than 2,000 years. The first rice plant came to Japan from China. It was considered a gift from the gods. Even today, rice plays a special role in Japanese life. It is the first solid food Japanese babies eat. It is the main source of nutrition for the sick. It is served at parties, weddings, and funerals. Rice is considered so essential that Japanese space shuttle astronauts carry a supply in space with them.

The Japanese are very particular about their rice. Not just any rice will do. It must be polished, white, and short grained. It also must be cooked perfectly. To the Japanese this means the rice must be carefully rinsed and soaked and then cooked until fluffy.

A Large Bowl of Rice

In the past, a typical Japanese meal often consisted of simply a bowl of rice. The Japanese still sometimes make a meal of rice. Most Japanese meals, however, consist of a large bowl of rice and several smaller dishes of other foods. These may be cooked and pickled vegetables or bite-size pieces of fish, chicken, squid, or shrimp. Sometimes fish broth or soy sauce is added to the rice for extra flavor. No matter what is served with it, rice is always the main part of every meal.

Sushi

Japanese Rice

The Japanese are very particular about their rice. They have been preparing it in the same way for hundreds of years. They use medium- or short-grain rice, and they never use instant rice. They always rinse the rice before cooking it.

Ingredients:

2 cups short- or medium-grain white rice
water for cleaning the rice
2 ¼ cups springwater

Instructions:

1. Put the rice in a large bowl and cover it with water.
2. Stir the rice around in the water with your clean hands.
3. Drain off the water.
4. Add more water and repeat the process.
5. Put the rice in a large pot. Cover the rice with the spring water. Let it soak for thirty minutes.
6. Put the pot on the stove and cook uncovered over medium heat until it starts to boil.
7. Lower the heat and cover the pot. Let the rice simmer until all the liquid is absorbed.
8. Remove the pot from the heat. Leave the cover on and do not disturb the rice. Let the pot stand this way for fifteen minutes.
9. Uncover the pot. Fluff the rice with a fork.
10. Put the rice into a big serving bowl and serve.

Makes 3 cups of rice

Rice is also an important ingredient in Japanese cooking. The Japanese put it in soup, stews, and sushi. They pour hot tea over it and eat it as Americans eat breakfast cereal. They make rice balls and rice cakes. They fry it, eat it cold, and make flour, vinegar, and wines with it. "Rice is the heart and soul of Japanese cuisine,"[1] explains Japanese cookbook author Susan Fuller Stack.

The Taste of a Hundred Things

To Japanese cooks, soybeans are almost as important an ingredient as rice. They eat them boiled and salted in a popular snack known as edamame. However, it is what they make from the beans that is essential to Japanese cooking.

Rice (close-up, inset) is Japan's most important food. Here, a Japanese farmer plants rice in a paddy.

Chopsticks

The Japanese eat their meals with chopsticks. That is why their food is always served in bite-size pieces.

Chopsticks can be plain or fancy. Everyday chopsticks may be made of bamboo or another wood. Special occasion chopsticks can be made of ivory or lacquered wood and inlaid with mother-of-pearl.

Each diner is given one set of chopsticks. Diners use the thick ends to serve themselves food from communal dishes. They use the thin ends to eat with.

Although there are not many rules about eating with chopsticks, certain behaviors are considered impolite. Pointing at someone with chopsticks is considered very rude. Spearing food with chopsticks and sticking chopsticks vertically into a bowl of rice are also considered impolite.

A sumo wrestler holds a bowl of rice close to his mouth as he eats with chopsticks.

Tofu is a snow-white block of soybean curd. Eaten alone, it has a delicate creamy taste. When cooked with other foods, tofu takes on their flavor. That may be why the Japanese say, "The taste of tofu is . . . the taste of a hundred things."[2]

The Japanese so love tofu that every neighborhood in Japan has at least one tofu shop where warm tofu is prepared fresh every morning. In some restaurants tofu is found in every dish on the menu. Dishes include soups with tofu, tofu with fish or rice, and a creamy tofu sherbet.

The Japanese use tofu in hundreds of ways. They broil it, bake it, fry it, steam it, **sauté** it, dry it, and freeze it. They make sauces and dressings from it. They put it in soup. On hot summer days, they eat it chilled covered with grated ginger and soy sauce. They sauté it with vegetables and flavor it with different sauces. Because tofu is loaded with protein, the Japanese use it in place of meat. In fact, it was 10th-century, vegetarian Buddhist monks who brought tofu from China to Japan.

Miso and Shoyu

The Japanese also use soybeans to make **miso** and **shoyu**, two ingredients used to flavor almost every Japanese dish. Miso is a tangy paste made by mixing steamed soybeans with koji, a fermenting agent that converts sugar to alcohol. It has a rich, salty flavor and a texture similar to peanut butter. The Japanese use miso as a topping for snacks, as a marinade for fish, to dress leafy vegetables, and to thicken and flavor sauces. They also use it to make miso soup, a favorite broth that is a combination of miso, fish **stock**, vegetables, tofu, pork, and seafood. To the Japanese, Chef Hiroko Shimbo explains, "Miso is mighty."[3]

Shoyu is another essential flavor. Known to North Americans as soy sauce, shoyu is made from soybeans, wheat, springwater, sea salt, and koji. It has a robust salty flavor, a fragrant aroma, and a rich brown color. The best shoyu is aged for up to two years before it is ready to eat.

The Japanese love shoyu. It is their number one seasoning. They say that its unique taste does not change the taste of food but instead brings out every food's individual flavor and natural sweetness. That is why they not only cook with shoyu, but also drizzle it on almost everything they eat. Shoyu is a popular dipping sauce, pickling agent, and marinade. Almost every Japanese recipe calls for shoyu. It is even used to make Japanese ice cream. A Japanese traveler returning from an overseas trip explains: "After eating meal after meal cooked with butter and oil, and flavored with salt and other Western condiments, what I missed the most was the flavor and aroma of shoyu."[4]

Foods from the Sea

Seafood is another favorite ingredient in Japanese cooking. It adds color and fresh flavor to the Japanese diet. Since ancient times, the waters surrounding Japan have provided the Japanese with a wide variety of

Chilled Tofu

Chilled tofu is a popular summer dish in Japan. It is very refreshing and easy to make.

Ingredients:

1 block tofu, chilled
2 green onions, sliced and chopped
2 tablespoons fresh grated ginger
24 ice cubes
soy sauce

Instructions:

1. Slice the tofu in half lengthwise. Put it on a plate and press another plate on top. Tilt the two plates, holding them over the sink, and let the excess water drain out.
2. When the tofu is drained, cut the tofu into 1-inch cubes.
3. Put the ice cubes in two soup bowls, about twelve in each.
4. Arrange the tofu cubes on top of the ice cubes.
5. Fill two small dipping bowls with soy sauce.
6. Put the ginger in a small bowl.
7. Put the green onions in a small bowl.
8. Give each person one bowl of iced tofu and one bowl of soy sauce.
9. Have diners dip the chilled tofu into the soy sauce and top the chilled tofu with as much ginger and green onions as they prefer.

Serves 2

seafood. Salmon, tuna, bonito, eel, shrimp, and squid are just a few of their favorites.

The Japanese eat seafood for breakfast, lunch, and dinner. They grill it, pickle it, steam it, make **sushi** with it, fill rice balls and dumplings with it, make a paste from it, use it in stews and soups, and eat it chilled, dried, and raw. Seafood is so popular that every day 4,000 tons (3,628 metric tons) of it are sold in Japan's largest city, Tokyo. Each Japanese person eats more than 150 pounds (68 kilograms) of seafood annually. According to Chef Jennifer Brennan, "Fish or seafood is eaten at every meal. It is unthinkable to prepare a Japanese meal without any of these."[5]

Seafood is abundant in Japan, as can be seen at this market where a man inspects frozen tuna for sale.

A worker in a Tokyo market carts a huge fish into the store. People in Tokyo eat thousands of tons of seafood every day.

Dashi

Another way the Japanese use seafood is to make **dashi**, a clear consommé, which the Japanese use as the basis for soups, stews, and sauces. Dashi is also the liquid that the Japanese prefer to use to cook and serve noodles in. Dashi is made from dried bonito fish and dried seaweed. It has a mild fishlike taste and a fragrance similar to the scent of the ocean.

The Japanese use so much dashi that instant dashi is sold in every Japanese supermarket. It is often packaged

たこ焼

This roadside food stand in Tokyo sells bowls of hot dashi soup with chunks of octopus.

inside tea bags that Japanese cooks dip into hot water. A typical dashi-based soup is likely to contain bits of fish, rice, vegetables, and tofu. It, as well as hundreds of other Japanese dishes, gets its delicious and unique flavors from seafood, rice, and soybeans. These three ingredients give Japanese food its distinct taste. They are the very roots of Japanese cooking.

chapter 2

A Feast for the Stomach and the Eyes

"**Y**ou eat with your eyes"[6] is an old Japanese saying. To the Japanese, cooking is an art. Their favorite foods—sushi, **tempura**, and **sukiyaki**—prove this. They are a perfect balance of taste, texture, and color.

Sushi

Sushi combines the Japanese peoples' love of fish and rice. It is made of scrumptious morsels of seafood that are pressed into cold rice seasoned with vinegar.

Salmon, tuna, octopus, crab, shrimp, and fish eggs are popular sushi ingredients. They may be cooked or smoked. More commonly, they are eaten raw. Sometimes thin slices of raw fish are served alone. This is called sashimi. No matter how the seafood is prepared, it is

This plate of sushi, a delicacy that combines cold rice with fish, makes for the perfect Japanese meal.

always extremely fresh. This keeps the sushi from tasting or smelling fishy or slimy. The rice is firm, and the fish is so tender that it practically melts in the mouth.

Different Shapes

Sushi comes in many forms. Traditional sushi, or nigiri-sushi, is made by pressing a slice of raw fish onto a bite-size portion of vinegar-flavored rice. Oshi-sushi is made by pressing rice topped with fish or seafood into a wooden mold and slicing it into tiny blocks. To make maki-sushi, cooks roll rice and fish into a long cylinder that is cut into round bite-size pieces. Often the rice is rolled between a sheet of delicious dried seaweed called **nori**, or nori is rolled around the rice mixture to form a little cone. The simplest of all sushi is chirashi-sushi. It consists of a bed of vinegar-flavored rice with thin slices of fish scattered decoratively on top.

The Sushi Master

Sushi originated as a way to preserve fish by fermenting it in rice. This gave the fish a sour flavor, which the Japanese loved. By the 1600s, the Japanese had replaced the fermenting process

A sushi master at a school for sushi chefs in Tokyo teaches his students how to remove the bones from a fish fillet.

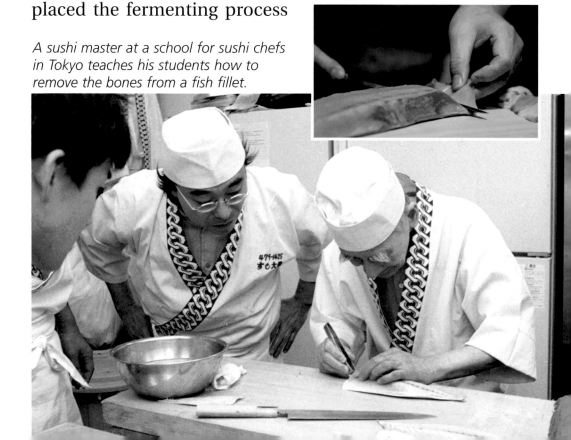

with vinegar. Today the Japanese are so passionate about sushi that there are about fifteen thousand sushi-yas—restaurants that serve nothing but sushi— in Tokyo alone. Here, chefs known as **sushi masters** stand behind very clean refrigerated glass counters filled with seafood. Diners give the sushi master their

Nigiri-Sushi

Making sushi takes a little practice, but it is not difficult. Nigiri-sushi is made by pressing a filling on an oval of rice. It is not rolled. This recipe calls for cooked shrimp for the filling, but any filling can be used. Avocado, salmon, lox, and tuna all make good fillings.

Ingredients:

3 cups of uncooked rice
$1/3$ cup rice vinegar
2 tablespoons sugar
$1/3$ teaspoon salt
water and vinegar for molding
$4\,1/2$ tablespoons wasabi paste or hot mustard
12 large cooked shrimp
soy sauce
pickled ginger

Instructions:

1. Cook the rice according to the package directions. Let the rice cool but do not refrigerate it.
2. Combine the vinegar, sugar, and salt. Put the mixture in a saucepan and cook over low heat until the sugar dissolves. Stir while cooking.

order. Then they watch as the master nimbly cuts and slices the fish and scoops up the precise amount of rice, all the while making sure that each rice kernel faces in the same direction.

The master arranges each mouthful on a plate along with a slice of pickled ginger and a dab of **wasabi**, which is

3. Pour the vinegar mixture over the rice and mix it in.
4. Combine one tablespoon of vinegar with one cup of water in a bowl.
5. Wet your clean hands with the vinegar-water mixture. Put about one and one-half tablespoons of rice into your palm. Press it gently to form an oblong or oval block smaller than the topping and about 1 inch thick.
6. Spread a little wasabi or hot mustard on the rice.
7. Put a shrimp over the wasabi or mustard. Press it into the rice, covering the rice completely.
8. Place soy sauce, pickled ginger, and additional wasabi or mustard on the table. Give each person a dipping bowl. Diners can make their own dipping sauce. Make sure there is enough pickled ginger so that each person gets one slice.

Makes 12 pieces of sushi

A group of Japanese students sitting in the park enjoys bento lunches of rice, vegetables, and fish.

a spicy, green Japanese horseradish. Diners mix the wasabi with shoyu to form a zesty dipping sauce. Bites of ginger add sweetness and refresh the palate. The combination of tastes and colors are wonderful. Dark green nori, snow-white rice, and coral salmon is an example of one beautiful and flavorful combination. Bright red tuna, pale green cucumber, and pure white rice is another. "Sushi," Japanese food and culture expert, Donald Richie, explains, "is a delight to the eye, and a revelation to the tongue."[7]

Golden Tempura

Tempura is another favorite Japanese dish that looks as good as it tastes. Tempura is made from vegetables and seafood such as scallops, squid, shrimp, eggplant, and

Japanese Meals

The Japanese eat three meals a day. Breakfast usually consists of rice, fish, and miso soup. It is usually eaten quite early.

Many Japanese workers and students carry a bento, or lunch box, with them. It is likely to contain a rice ball or a casserole of rice with different vegetables and fish. Noodles are another popular lunch.

Supper is the largest meal of the day. It always contains rice. Soup, sushi, tempura, sukiyaki, stew, vegetables, fish, seafood, or chicken may be served with the rice. Dessert is usually a small serving of seasonal fruit. A few grapes or a sliver of melon is popular. It is followed by a cup of green tea, which is never served with the meal. Instead, it is served afterward.

Some Japanese people eat their meals at traditional low tables sitting on cushions placed on the floor. Most modern Japanese people eat at Western-style tables and chairs.

The traditional Japanese breakfast features miso soup, rice, and fish.

Tempura

mushrooms. They are dipped into batter and then fried until golden.

Tempura has been a favorite food in Japan since the 16th century, when Portuguese missionaries introduced deep-fried breaded fish to the Japanese.

Over the centuries the Japanese adapted the recipe to make it their own. Unlike most deep-fried foods that are popular in America and Europe, tempura is not heavy or greasy. Instead it is almost totally grease free, and it is light as a feather. Tempura, according to a Web site devoted to Japanese cuisine, "is one of the triumphs of Japanese cooking—a fried food that is light and fresh tasting."[8]

A Careful Process

Preparing tempura takes skill and practice. The batter must be the perfect consistency. The oil temperature must be exact, and the tempura must be cooked for just the right amount of time.

To make tempura, the cook first cuts bite-size pieces of seafood and vegetables. As with sushi, only the freshest ingredients are used. Sometimes live shrimp kept in a pail of water go right into the frying pan.

Next the cook makes a batter from ice water, eggs, and flour. To keep the tempura from tasting greasy, the batter is not mixed thoroughly. Lumps in the batter contain air

So Lifelike You Could Eat Them

Most Japanese restaurants display delicious samples of their food in their windows. These samples tempt hungry diners and passersby. Although they sit in the windows for hours, they never spoil. This is because they are not real. They are made from wax or plastic. They are so lifelike that it is difficult to distinguish them from real food.

To make lifelike food out of wax, an artist creates a mold in the shape of the food. The wax is poured into the mold. When the wax is set, it is colored to look like the real food. With such attention to detail, making one piece of wax food can take a month. The Japanese are considered masters in making food replicas.

Although these foods displayed in a Japanese restaurant window look good enough to eat, they are actually made of plastic.

An Okinawan father uses chopsticks to feed his toddler bits of tempura and rice.

bubbles, which prevent the tempura from absorbing too much oil. Because the air bubbles disappear as the batter starts to settle, only a small amount of batter is used at a time.

The cook carefully dips the seafood and vegetables into the batter. The coating must be so thin that it is almost see-through. This keeps the flavor of the breading from overwhelming the taste of the seafood or vegetables.

The ingredients are then dropped into a pan of hot oil, which is kept at about 340°F (170°C). If the oil is too hot, the tempura will burn. If it is not hot enough, the seafood will not cook thoroughly.

The tempura is cooked for about two minutes. It is served hot with rice and a dipping sauce made from dashi, ginger, and grated radish. Perfect tempura is yummy— crunchy on the outside and tender and juicy on the inside.

Sukiyaki: A Communal Meal

Sukiyaki is another of the Japanese people's favorite foods. Sukiyaki is a type of **nabemono**, or stew. Unlike American-style stew, sukiyaki is made right on the dinner table.

To make sukiyaki, a heated cooking ring is placed on the table. A pan similar to a cast-iron skillet sits on top of it. Then the ingredients are added. Thin slices of beef artistically arranged to form a flower pattern fill one platter. Other platters filled with bite-size pieces of fresh tofu, mushrooms, pea pods, bean sprouts, onions, clear gelatinous noodles, and chrysanthemum leaves surround the meat.

Small bowls containing sweetened shoyu are set before each diner, along with a raw egg. Now the fun begins.

First, a piece of fat is melted in the hot pan. The beef slices follow with the tofu and vegetables on top of them. When the meat starts to brown, the sweetened shoyu is poured in. Meanwhile the cook, and often all the diners,

Sukiyaki

Sukiyaki is usually made at the table in an electric frying pan or in a cast-iron frying pan placed over a portable burner. If this is unavailable, sukiyaki can be prepared on the stove and brought to the table cooked. In that case, the cook removes the cooked ingredients from the pan. Serve sukiyaki with rice and dipping bowls of soy sauce.

Ingredients:

4 green onions, cut into 1-inch slices
6 mushrooms, sliced
half a carrot, sliced thin
6 ounces firm tofu, cut into 1-inch cubes
1 pound lean sirloin beef cut into wafer-thin slices
3/4 cup soy sauce
1/3 cup sugar
3/4 cup beef or chicken consommé
2 1/2 tablespoons vegetable oil
4 eggs (optional)
6 ounces napa (Chinese) cabbage, sliced

Instructions:

1. Wash and slice the vegetables. Arrange the vegetables and tofu on a plate. Take to the table.

stirs the sukiyaki with chopsticks so that it cooks evenly.

Cooking time is very brief. The meat is done when it just starts to turn brown, and the other ingredients barely cook at all. Diners serve themselves. They pick their favorite foods out of the cooking pot and place them over a bowl of rice. At the same time, they break their eggs into

2. Arrange the beef on another plate in a flower pattern. Take to the table.
3. Combine the soy sauce, sugar, and consommé in a saucepan and cook on low heat, mixing until the sugar dissolves. Remove from the heat. Take the sauce to the table.
4. At the table, heat the oil in the skillet.
5. Put in a layer of beef. Cook the beef without stirring for one minute.
6. Add a layer of the vegetables and tofu.
7. Pour enough soy sauce mixture over the beef and vegetables to cover them.
8. Have diners remove the foods from the pan as they are done.
9. As the food is removed from the pan, add more food and repeat the cooking procedures.

Serves 4

Three generations of a Japanese family sit on floor cushions at a traditional low table as they enjoy a meal of sushi together.

their bowls of sweetened shoyu and stir the mixture with their chopsticks. Before eating, they dip the sukiyaki into the sauce. The heat of the beef, tofu, and vegetables causes the egg to become sticky. When the sukiyaki is dipped into the sauce, the sauce sticks to it to form a sweet coating. The results are heavenly. "The taste is unique, a combination of qualities that once experienced is not to be forgotten,"[9] Richie explains.

Once a person has tried them, he or she cannot forget the mouth-watering taste, enticing aroma, and beautiful appearance of sukiyaki, tempura, and sushi. It is no wonder they are favorite foods in Japan.

Chapter 3

Snacks and Treats

The Japanese love to snack. Restaurants, convenience stores, teahouses, and street vendors tempt people with hundreds of unique treats. Among everyone's favorites are rice balls, noodles, green tea, and tea sweets.

Rice Balls

Onigiri, or rice balls, have been a favorite Japanese snack for centuries. Rice balls are snow-white mounds of rice filled with anything and everything. Smoked salmon, tuna, shrimp, fish eggs, and pickled plums are popular fillings. They may be used alone or combined with other fillings such as mayonnaise, scrambled egg, or red pepper flakes.

Cooks in the kitchen of a busy restaurant in Kyoto prepare skewers of rice balls, a favorite Japanese snack.

A rice ball's flavor depends on the filling. Filled with shrimp and mayonnaise, it tastes like seafood salad. Filled with fish eggs and red pepper, it is hot and spicy. The Japanese make so many different flavors of rice balls, there is one to suit everyone's taste.

To make rice balls, cooks place about one-quarter cup hot rice into their hands. They make a dent in the middle of the rice and fill it with the ingredients of their choice. Then they add more rice to the rice ball and shape it into a sphere or triangle. To make the rice ball crunchy, they may roll it in sesame seeds. Then cooks wrap the rice ball with strips of nori, which help hold it together.

Foods of Japan

Rice Balls

Making rice balls is not difficult. They can be filled with almost anything. This recipe uses canned salmon. Tuna fish, grilled salmon, and crab all make good fillings too.

Ingredients:

1 pound rice
1 7.5-ounce can salmon
water
1 teaspoon salt
2 sheets of nori, cut into 12 strips

Instructions:

1. Cook the rice according to the directions on the package. Let the rice cool slightly. To make the rice balls, the rice should still be hot, but not too hot to handle.
2. Take the salmon out of the can and drain the liquid. Break up the salmon into twelve loose chunks.
3. Fill a small bowl with cold water. Add the salt and stir.
4. Put two tablespoons of rice into a teacup. With your clean fingers, make a small hollow in the middle of the rice. Put one of the salmon chunks in the hollow. Cover the salmon with one tablespoon of rice.
5. Wet your hands with the saltwater. Holding the teacup over one hand, turn it upside down so that the rice in the teacup comes out in your hand.
6. Squeeze the rice, shaping it into a firm ball.
7. Wrap a strip of nori around the rice ball.
8. Repeat until all the rice and salmon are used.

Makes 12 rice balls

The Proper Way to Eat Noodles

Although the Japanese usually consider it impolite to make noises while eating, the opposite is true when it comes to eating noodles. The Japanese consider it polite to make loud slurping and smacking sounds while eating them. When they are served a bowl of noodles, the Japanese move the bowl close to their mouths. This makes it easy to eat with chopsticks without bits of food falling into the diner's lap. The Japanese lift the noodles from the bowl with their chopsticks and then suck the noodles down. When the noodles are gone, rather than spooning the broth into their mouths, they bring the bowl to their mouth and drink the broth.

This Japanese man shows the right way to eat noodles, by holding the bowl close to his mouth and slurping the noodles up.

Steam from noodles and soup fogs up the interior of a ramen shop in Osaka.

A Portable Snack

Rice balls are perfect on-the-go snacks that taste great. This may be why ancient Japanese travelers always carried rice balls with them. Today, Japanese children munch on rice balls as they play in parks and school yards, and Japanese adults devour them as they go about their busy lives. Rice balls take the place of hot dogs at Japanese baseball games and fill the shelves of convenience stores. Mimi, a Japanese woman, explains: "Onigiri is one of my top comfort foods. It reminds me of the ones my mother used to make for me for school outings as well as countless school lunches."[10]

Noodles

Menrui, or noodles, are the Japanese people's favorite fast food. Noodle shops can be found everywhere. At lunchtime they are packed with busy business people enjoying a quick bowl of noodles. Street vendors and convenience stores also offer different noodle dishes twenty-four hours a day. When it comes to noodles, authors John Ashburne and Yoshi Abe explain, "Everyone has a favorite restaurant, a favorite dish, a favorite stock, even a favorite convenience store variety."[11]

The Japanese make three kinds of noodles—**soba**, **udon**, and **ramen**. All three were brought to Japan from China in the 16th century. Soba is a long gray noodle made from buckwheat, which gives it a hearty taste. Udon is a white noodle that can be long, round, square, or flat. It is made from ordinary wheat, as is ramen. However, eggs are used to make ramen, which give it a yellow color. Both ramen and udon taste lighter and more delicate than soba.

All three noodles may be prepared fresh or dried. Ramen is often sold in dried, instant form with a packet of dashi- or shoyu-based flavoring. Diners just add hot water.

Hot or Cold

The Japanese serve noodles in hundreds of ways. They eat them hot or cold, with dipping sauce, in soup, or topped

Kake Soba

Kake soba is soba noodles in broth. Dried soba noodles are sold in Asian food stores and in some supermarkets and health food stores. Udon or ramen noodles can also be used. The broth uses instant dashi, which is sold in Asian food stores. Chicken consommé can be used instead of the dashi broth.

Ingredients:

1 pound dried soba noodles
4 cups water
3 teaspoons instant dashi
4 green onions, sliced thin
2 tablespoons grated ginger

Instructions:

1. Fill a large pot with water. There should be four times as much water as noodles. Bring the water to a boil.
2. Put the noodles in the boiling water and stir. After the water starts to boil again, lower the heat and let the noodles cook for about seven minutes, or according to the package directions.
3. Remove the pot from the stove, strain the water.
4. Put the four cups of water in a pot and bring to a boil. When the water boils, add the instant dashi and stir.
5. Divide the soba noodles among four bowls.
6. Pour one cup of broth into each bowl.
7. Sprinkle with sliced green onion and ginger.

Serves 4

Green Tea

with fish, chicken, vegetables, tofu, or tempura. In winter, hot udon served in miso soup with shrimp, fried tofu, mixed vegetables, and a raw egg cracked over the top is quite popular. When the weather gets hot, the Japanese cool down with cold noodles, which they dip into a sweet shoyu sauce. Sesame seeds, grated ginger, and nori are popular accompaniments.

The Japanese are so passionate about noodles that they have more than one dozen noodle museums. Exhibits give information about the history of noodles, show how noodles are made, and display noodle-making utensils. One museum even boasts a noodle theme park!

Ocha

When the Japanese want to quench their thirst, **ocha**, or green tea, is their favorite drink. No meal or snack is complete without this pale green liquid. In fact, a fresh steamy cup of green tea is satisfying all by itself.

Unlike tea drinkers in other countries, the Japanese never add milk, sugar, or lemon to their tea. They do not want to change its natural taste. Nor do they drink iced tea or tea made from boiling water. If the water is too cold or too hot, the Japanese say, it ruins the taste of the tea. Instead they heat water to about 175°F (80°C) and then steep the tea for less than one minute. If the tea steeps too long, it

A woman dressed in traditional clothing prepares tea in a traditional tea ceremony, a complex ritual that is centuries old.

becomes too strong to suit their taste. The Japanese like their tea to have a delicate bittersweet flavor that remains in the mouth long after the teacup is drained. "The last cup of tea is drunk," Richie explains. But, "the taste of Japan, fresh, natural, slightly astringent, still lingers."[12]

Chagashi Instead of Sugar

Green tea is refreshing but slightly bitter. That may be why the Japanese like to eat **chagashi**, or tea sweets, with their tea. Tea sweets are Japanese pastries. Unlike Western-style pastries, tea sweets are not baked. They are **steamed**. Also, rather than being made from wheat flour, eggs, and butter, their main ingredients are rice flour, sugar, and sweet mild-tasting **azuki beans**.

To make tea sweets, Japanese bakers make dough from rice flour, sugar, and water. They fill the dough with red or white azuki beans that have been boiled and mashed into a paste. Sometimes sticky rice or yams are also used as fillings. Each gives the tea sweet a different color and flavor. It may be pink, white, or yellow.

The filled dough is cooked in a special steamer basket, which is placed over a pot of boiling water. The result is a soft spongy cake with a delicious, light flavor.

A Sweet for Every Season

Tea sweets are made in dozens of different shapes. Most are quite delicate and beautiful. Formed to reflect the season, their appearance depends on the time of year. For example, a popular spring sweet is shaped like a kimono and stamped with a crest that looks like a

The Legend of the First Tea Plant

Tea was introduced to Japan around A.D. 800. Most experts think monks brought the drink to Japan from China. An ancient Japanese legend credits one of these monks for giving the Japanese their first tea plant. It seems rather than sleep at night, this monk prayed. One night he felt so sleepy that he tore off his eyelids in order to keep them from closing. Then he threw them out the window. The next morning a tea plant, the leaves of which are shaped like eyelids, grew outside his window. From then on the monk had plenty of tea and did not have to worry about falling asleep.

Farm workers on a tea plantation on the island of Kyushu take a break from the hard work of picking tea leaves.

An artist painstakingly decorates a steamed tea sweet with the colors of the season

cherry blossom. Winter sweets are pure white on the outside and shaped to look like tiny snowballs. Sweets made in the form of pink chrysanthemum flowers are an autumn favorite.

Although the look of the sweets changes with the season, the ingredients remain the same. Shimbo explains: "The traditional sweets sold in Japanese stores appear different depending on the time of year. They are shaped into various flowers, fruits, birds, fish, and scenery to give a strong sense of the season. But only the forms and colors of the sweets change, not their tastes."[13]

No matter their shape, tea sweets always taste delicious. So do noodles, rice balls, and green tea. It is no wonder the Japanese love to snack.

Chapter 4

Foods for Celebrations

The Japanese love to celebrate. Holidays and festivals fill their calendar. Special foods with special meanings make these celebrations wonderful.

Lucky Soup

New Year's Day is the most important of all Japanese holidays. In the days leading up to January 1, the Japanese build little altars in their homes, which they decorate with small towers made of rice cakes. The rice cakes' round shape symbolizes wealth, and their snow-white color represents the purity of the New Year. The Japanese say that eating these rice cakes for breakfast on New Year's Day in a soup called **ozoni** brings them wealth and happiness in the coming year. Donna, a woman married to a Japanese man, explains: "It doesn't feel right if we don't eat ozoni on New Year's Day."[14]

The Japanese make many different varieties of ozoni, depending on the part of Japan in which it is made. In Tokyo, ozoni is made like chicken soup. In Osaka, it is made like miso soup. The vegetables, fish, and meat that go in the ozoni also vary. Chicken, mushrooms, onions, radishes, and fish are just a few of the most popular

A farmer uses a heavy wooden mallet to pound steamed rice into mochi paste, while his wife stirs the mixture.

Sweet Black Beans

Kuromame, or sweet black beans, are always included in the New Year's jubako. Because the beans are dried, they take time to prepare. They are not difficult to make, however.

Ingredients:

3 cups water
2 teaspoons soy sauce
$3/4$ cup sugar
$1/2$ teaspoon salt
$1/2$ teaspoon baking soda
1 cup dried black beans

Instructions:

1. Combine the water, soy sauce, sugar, salt, and baking soda in a pot and bring it to a boil. Stir the mixture while it is cooking.
2. When the sugar has dissolved, remove the pot from the heat and let the mixture cool.
3. When the mixture is cool, add the beans. Let the beans soak for about eight hours.
4. Place the pot on the stove. Cover and cook on low heat until the beans are soft, about four to six hours.
5. Let the beans cool before serving.

Serves 6

ingredients. Despite regional differences, all ozoni contains rice cakes, which the soup is poured over.

Making Mochi

Mochi, or rice cakes, are made from sticky rice that is steamed and then pounded into a paste while it is still warm. Pounding mochi takes a lot of strength. First, Japanese cooks pour hot rice onto a large mortar made from wood or concrete. Then they pound the rice with a big wooden mallet. The pounding takes a long time. Cooks continue pounding until the rice forms a smooth, shiny mass in which no individual grains are visible. Because the rice must be turned repeatedly while it is being pounded, it takes at least two people to do the job.

In the past, pounding mochi was a traditional New Year activity for Japanese families. Today there are machines that pound mochi. Around New Year's, however, Japanese sumo wrestlers and baseball players often appear on television doing the job.

In a Kyoto food shop, a worker places a paste of red azuki beans between layers of mochi.

When the mochi is ready, it is formed into flat buns. Mochi is dense and sticky with a texture similar to peanut butter. When it is put in ozoni, it turns slippery and becomes easy to eat. Not only that, it tastes fantastic.

A Cook's Holiday

The New Year's celebration does not end on New Year's Day. It continues through January 3. The Japanese want the first few days of January to be happy and stress free. If they are, they say, the rest of the year will also be happy. That is why no one works during this time. To ensure that everyone, including the cook, has a relaxing holiday, most people buy ready-made boxes of traditional New Year's food or **osechi-ryori** to feast on.

Osechi-ryori is a special selection of 20 to 30 Japanese dishes that are grouped together only at New Year's. Sold in supermarkets, department stores, and restaurants, osechi-ryori comes in a **jubako**, an elaborately arranged collection of layered boxes. Each little box is filled with a different ready-made food item.

Inside the Jubako

A typical jubako contains a mix of different seafood, vegetables, and

Foods with special meanings for the New Year include seafood and vegetables.

Wearing a kimono, a Japanese saleswoman holds a beautiful jubako box filled with delicious osechi-ryori.

egg dishes. Each is carefully packaged and arranged with other foods of complementary colors, smells, and tastes. Each food has a special meaning. Because osechi-ryori is eaten right from the box, most of the food is made with lots of sugar, shoyu, and vinegar, all of which prevent spoilage.

Inside the jubako, the boxes nest like little shelves. The top shelf contains appetizers such as black beans boiled in sweet syrup. Black beans are linked to good health. Sweet chestnuts, sweet potatoes, and an omelet rolled up to look like a scroll also can be found in this layer. The chestnuts and potatoes symbolize success, and the omelet represents knowledge.

Food Shopping in Japan

When the Japanese shop for holiday foods, they have a big choice of stores that they can visit. Specialty stores are everywhere. There are stores that sell only dried fish and vegetables and other stores that sell only pickled foods. Other stores sell nothing but fruit, some of which are gift wrapped for holiday gift giving. Junk sweet shops sell only cheap candies, and tofu stores sell fresh tofu. Convenience stores sell packaged food. Even department stores offer a wide variety of foods.

For the biggest selection, the Japanese head to supermarkets. Japanese supermarkets are large, brightly lit, super clean, and noisy. Taped music and announcements loudly urge shoppers "to buy, buy, buy."

Japanese shoppers have many foods to choose from. There are all kinds of fruits and vegetables, and they are all perfect. Bruised produce is not sold. There are separate sections for pickles, tofu, and noodles. Noodles come with prepackaged dips. The seafood section is huge. Here shoppers can find every seafood imaginable. The meat section offers beef imported from the United States and Australia. Japanese beef is also offered. It is three to four times more expensive than imported beef.

The second shelf is usually filled with bite-size bits of different types of seafood such as lobster and prawns, both of which stand for long life, and sea bream, which is associated with fun and celebration. These are main dishes.

The third and fourth layers hold vegetables that are often beautifully arranged to form a pine cone or a plum blossom. Many are pickled. The root vegetables, such as radishes, carrots, and burdock root stand for stability, because their roots are planted firmly in the earth.

When the Japanese eat the foods in the jubako, they hope their special meanings will follow them into the New Year. Even if the foods do not bring them strength or wealth, eating osechi-ryori is a New Year's tradition in Japan. Author Blake More explains: "Osechi-ryori can be viewed as the national cuisine of New Year's, kind of like turkey and cranberries are to America's Thanksgiving."[15]

Festive Stir-Fry

The Japanese celebrate not only on holidays such as New Year's, they have many festivals throughout the year. Some festivals such as Children's Day honor people. Others, such

Barrels full of fresh produce straight from the farm entice shoppers at a market in Kyoto.

as the Cherry Blossom Festival and the Harvest Moon Festival, celebrate nature. Each festival gives the Japanese people another chance to have fun outdoors and to eat **yakisoba**, their favorite festival food.

Yakisoba is made from steamed noodles that are prepared with a variety of ingredients. Pork, shrimp, squid, boiled eggs, tofu, bamboo shoots, mushrooms, cabbage, and carrots are some of the most popular.

Speed and Skill

Yakisoba is almost always made outdoors at little stands equipped with an iron griddle and a steamer basket. Cooks stand behind the griddle where they rapidly slice the ingredients. Then they throw the ingredients and freshly steamed noodles onto the hot, oiled griddle. Holding a spatula in each hand, they rapidly turn and toss the ingredients around the griddle so that everything cooks evenly. This procedure is known as **stir-frying** and was developed in China.

To stir-fry effectively, cooks must coat the griddle with oil and preheat it until it is very hot. This prevents the food from sticking. All the ingredients must be cut into small, equal-size pieces, so that they cook at about the same time, which is not long at all. Cooking time is usually less than five minutes.

When the yakisoba is almost done, cooks pour a special sauce made from shoyu, **mirin**, and sugar onto the griddle rather than over the ingredients. This causes the sauce to burn and fill the air with an incredible aroma. It also delicately flavors the yakisoba.

Yakisoba

Yakisoba is easy to make. If soba noodles are not available, use ramen noodles.

Ingredients:

8 ounces soba or ramen noodles
1/4 cup soy sauce
3 tablespoons sugar
3 tablespoons vegetable oil
1 bunch green onions, minced
1 cup bean sprouts
1 teaspoon grated ginger
2 cups green cabbage leaves, chopped

Instructions:

1. Cook the noodles according to the package directions.
2. Drain the cooked noodles.
3. Combine the soy sauce and sugar in a saucepan. Cook on low heat until the sugar dissolves, stirring constantly.
4. Put the oil in a deep frying pan or a wok. Heat over medium heat.
5. Add the green onions, bean sprouts, ginger, and cabbage to the pan. Stir-fry for two minutes.
6. Add the noodles and soy sauce mixture. Stir-fry for one minute.
7. Turn off the heat. Cover the pot and let it sit for two minutes.

Serves 2

Crisp or Soft

Yakisoba can have soft or crunchy noodles. If the noodles are stir-fried with the other ingredients, they are soft. To make the noodles crispy, cooks deep-fry them separately, then add them to the stir-fried ingredients at the last minute. Whether soft or chewy, yakisoba is usually served with pickled ginger and seaweed flakes. Eaten with yak-

A Food to Fight the Heat

Although the New Year's celebration is the most important annual event in Japan, the Japanese celebrate year-round. One special day, the Day of the Ox, is celebrated at the end of July. This day is said to be the hottest day of the year. To fight the heat, the Japanese eat unagi, or eel. Eating eel, they believe, cools and strengthens the body. This helps people to fight heat exhaustion and, the Japanese say, gives them vitality for the rest of the year. Scientists do not know if this is true. Eel is very nutritious. It is loaded with vitamins A and E—two nutrients that are essential for good health.

Eel has always been a popular food in Japan. In fact, the Japanese people eat about 75,000 pounds of eel a year, and much of it is consumed on the Day of the Ox.

These Japanese flight attendants brought back live eels from Taiwan to prepare as the main dish for their Day of the Ox feast.

isoba, these ingredients add a sweet and sour taste. The final result is a dish that Japanese festival-goers cannot resist. Says Shimbo: "If you visit any festival in Japan, you will find a yakisoba food stall. . . . No one can pass by without buying the noodles or, at least, stopping to savor the delicious smell. The aroma of frying yakisoba noodles is the nostalgic smell of a Japanese street festival!"[16]

Whether it is with the aroma of yakisoba, the great taste of a steamy bowl of ozoni, or the beauty of osechi-ryori, Japanese celebrations are marked with special foods. Their great flavors and special meanings make festive occasions memorable.

Mass (weight)

1 ounce (oz.)	= 28.0 grams (g)
8 ounces	= 227.0 grams
1 pound (lb.) or 16 ounces	= 0.45 kilograms (kg)
2.2 pounds	= 1.0 kilogram

Liquid Volume

1 teaspoon (tsp.)	= 5.0 milliliters (ml)
1 tablespoon (tbsp.)	= 15.0 milliliters
1 fluid ounce (oz.)	= 30.0 milliliters
1 cup (c.)	= 240 milliliters
1 pint (pt.)	= 480 milliliters
1 quart (qt.)	= 0.95 liters (l)
1 gallon (gal.)	= 3.80 liters

Pan Sizes

8-inch cake pan	= 20 x 4-centimeter cake pan
9-inch cake pan	= 23 x 3.5-centimeter cake pan
11 x 7-inch baking pan	= 28 x 18-centimeter baking pan
13 x 9-inch baking pan	= 32.5 x 23-centimeter baking pan
9 x 5-inch loaf pan	= 23 x 13-centimeter loaf pan
2-quart casserole	= 2-liter casserole

Temperature

212° F	= 100° C (boiling point of water)
225° F	= 110° C
250° F	= 120° C
275° F	= 135° C
300° F	= 150° C
325° F	= 160° C
350° F	= 180° C
375° F	= 190° C
400° F	= 200° C

Length

1/4 inch (in.)	= 0.6 centimeters (cm)
1/2 inch	= 1.25 centimeters
1 inch	= 2.5 centimeters

Notes

Chapter 1: The Roots of Japanese Cooking

1. Susan Fuller Stack, *Japanese Cooking for the American Table.* New York: HP, 1996, p. 191.
2. Quoted in Donald Richie, *A Taste of Japan.* Tokyo: Kodansha International, 1985, p. 34.
3. Hiroko Shimbo, *The Japanese Kitchen.* Boston: Harvard Common Press, 2000, p. 81.
4. Quoted in Shimbo, *The Japanese Kitchen,* p. 89.
5. Jennifer Brennan, *The Cuisines of Asia.* New York: St. Martin's, 1984, p. 43.

Chapter 2: A Feast for the Stomach and the Eyes

6. Quoted in Shunsuke Fukushima, *Japanese Home Cooking.* Boston: Periplus Editions (HK), 2001, p. 36.
7. Richie, *A Taste of Japan,* p. 14.
8. Quoted in Bento.com, "Tempura." www.bento.com/re_temp.html.
9. Richie, *A Taste of Japan,* p. 21.

Chapter 3: Snacks and Treats

10. Quoted in I Was Just Really Very Hungry, "Onigiri (rice balls)." http://maki.typepad.com/justhungry/2003/12/obento.html.

11. John Ashburne and Yoshi Abe, *World Food Japan.* Victoria, Australia: Lonely Planet, 2002, p. 37.
12. Richie, *A Taste of Japan,* p. 109.
13. Shimbo, *The Japanese Kitchen,* p. 95.

Chapter 4: Foods for Celebrations

14. Quoted in eye Candy, "Mochi Celebrates the Season." http://visuals.champuru.com/archives/2002_12_29_index.html.
15. Blake More, "Osechi Ryori: The Art of New Years Cuisine," (from Tradepia International). www.snakelyone.com/osechi.htm.
16. Shimbo, *The Japanese Kitchen,* p. 158.

Glossary

azuki beans: Sweet beans that the Japanese use to make pastries.

chagashi: Steamed pastries eaten with tea.

dashi: Consommé made from dried bonito fish and kelp.

jubako: A collection of layered lacquered boxes that contain osechi-ryori.

menrui: The Japanese word for noodles.

mirin: A sweet Japanese wine made from rice.

miso: A paste made from fermented soybeans.

mochi: Sticky rice cakes.

nabemono: Japanese word for stew.

nori: A type of seaweed popular in Japan.

ocha: Green tea.

onigiri: A ball of rice filled with fish, vegetables, or other ingredients and eaten as a snack.

osechi-ryori: A combination of foods that is served on the first three days of January.

ozoni: A soup made with rice cakes that is served on New Year's Day.

ramen: A yellow egg noodle.

sauté: To lightly fry.

shoyu: A sauce made from fermented soybeans. It is also called soy sauce.

soba: A long gray noodle made from buckwheat.

steamed: Cooked with the steam of boiling water.

stir-frying: Frying rapidly while tossing and stirring the food.

stock: Fish, beef, chicken, or vegetable consommé.

sukiyaki: A beef and vegetable stew.

sushi: Morsels of seafood and vegetables that are pressed into cold rice seasoned with vinegar.

sushi master: Sushi chef.

tempura: Breaded and fried seafood and vegetables.

udon: A white noodle.

wasabi: A spicy green Japanese horseradish served with sushi.

yakisoba: A stir-fried noodle dish usually served at festivals.

For Further Exploration

Books

Theresa M. Beatty, *Food and Recipes of Japan.* New York: Powerhouse, 1999. This is a Japanese cookbook for kids.

Bobbie Kalman, *Japan.* New York: Crabtree, 2000. This book includes information about Japan's geography, history, and natural resources.

Julie McCulloch, *Japan (World of Recipes).* Chicago: Heinemann Library, 2001. This is a Japanese cookbook for kids.

Kaoru Ono, *Sushi for Kids: Children's Introduction to Japan's Favorite Food.* Rutland, VT: Tuttle, 2003. This book gives facts, recipes, and pictures of sushi.

Shozo Sato, *Tea Ceremony.* Rutland, VT: Tuttle, 2005. This book talks about tea and the Japanese tea ceremony.

Mari Takabayashi, *I Live in Tokyo.* Boston: Houghton Mifflin, 2001. Mimiko, a Japanese girl, talks about her life. The book includes information about her favorite foods, snacks, and festivals.

Web Sites

A Girl's World (www.agirlsworld.com/amy/pajama/childrensday). This Web site provides links to information about, and photos of, Japanese dolls, arts and crafts, music, dance, anime, and the Osaka Aquarium.

Thinkquest (www.thinkquest.org/library/cat_show.html?cat_id=211). Besides its many other offerings, this Web site offers links to games and information about Japan developed by young people. These include a virtual Japanese restaurant.

Web Japan (http://web-japan.org/kidsweb/cook.html). This site offers an online Japanese cookbook for children.

The World of Kikkoman (http://kikkoman.com/edu1.html). This soy sauce manufacturer has a special Web site for children. It gives simple recipes and facts about soy sauce and has electronic postcards made by Japanese children that Web site visitors can send.

Index